Governor Zell Miller's
Reading Initiative

Dolley Payne Todd Madison

Dolley Payne Todd Madison

* * * * * * * * * * * * * * * * * * *

1768-1849

BY ALICE K. FLANAGAN

CHILDREN'S PRESS®
A Division of Grolier Publishing
New York   London   Hong Kong   Sydney
Danbury, Connecticut

FOR H.M.N., WHO SO RESEMBLES DOLLEY

Consultants: KENNETH M. CLARK
                President, James Madison Memorial Foundation and Museum
                LINDA CORNWELL
                Learning Resource Consultant
                Indiana Department of Education

Project Editor: DOWNING PUBLISHING SERVICES
Page Makeup: CAROLE DESNOES
Photo Research: JAN IZZO

Library of Congress Cataloging in Publication Data
Flanagan, Alice.
        Dolley Payne Todd Madison / by Alice K. Flanagan.
            p.   cm. — (Encyclopedia of First ladies)
        Includes bibliographical references and index.
        Summary: A biography of the fourth First Lady, who had tremendous influence on
the social and political life of early America.
        ISBN 0-516-20642-7
        1. Madison, Dolley, 1768–1849—Juvenile literature.   2. Presidents' spouses—United
States—Biography—Juvenile literature.   3. Madison, James, 1751–1836 —Juvenile
literature.   4. United States —Politics and government—1809–1817—Juvenile literature.
[1. Madison, Dolley, 1768–1849.   2. First ladies.   3. Women—Biography.]   I. Title.
II. Series.
E342.1.F58   1997
973.5'1'092—dc21   97–21380
[B]   CIP
                                                                    AC

Table of Contents

Dolley Payne Todd Madison

The Legendary Dolley

* ☆ ☆ ☆ ☆ ☆ ☆ ☆ ☆ ☆ ☆ ☆ ☆ ☆ ☆ ☆ ☆ *

Few First Ladies had more influence on the social and political life of early America than Dolley Payne Todd Madison. As the wife of the fourth president of the United States, she played a key role in the development of the new nation's character and the quality of its public image.

Dolley Madison knew all of the presidents from George Washington to Zachary Taylor. She served as the White House hostess for President Thomas Jefferson. She was official hostess during her husband's two terms in office. Until she died in 1849, Dolley was involved in the social life of Washington, D.C.

☆ ☆ ☆ ☆ ☆ ☆ ☆ ☆ ☆ ☆ ☆ ☆ ☆ ☆ ☆ ☆

During the British invasion of Washington, D.C., in 1814, Dolley Madison rescued what she could from the White House.

Almost singlehandedly, Dolley Madison defined the role of First Lady. She set the standards for fashion and social manners in the capital for more than sixteen years. Dolley was a model of European fashion and elegance in an age when pioneer ruggedness was the custom in America. Her charm and graciousness brought together groups of political rivals at a time when their differences threatened to change the course of history. Because of her courage and forethought during the British invasion of Washington, D.C., in 1814, some of America's finest national treasures have been preserved, including many state papers and a portrait of George Washington.

The British invasion of Washington, D.C., in 1814

CHAPTER ONE

A Proper Quaker Daughter

* * * * * * * * * * * * * * *

John and Mary Coles Payne were delighted when their daughter Dolley was born on May 20, 1768. She was their third child and the first girl. As such, Dolley received a great deal of attention. Her happy nature flowered under the Paynes' guidance and love.

Dolley was born in Guilford, North Carolina. When she was less than a year old, the family returned to Virginia, where they had once lived. Dolley's father reclaimed the small plantation at Bird Creek, near his wife's family. Both of Dolley's parents were clerks in the Cedar Creek Meeting of Friends, a religious group known as the Quakers. As clerks, the Paynes conduct-

* * * * * * * * * * * * * * *

These Quakers on their way to a Sunday morning meeting were dressed in traditional plain clothing.

In about 1770, when Dolley was almost two, the Paynes bought an old estate called Scotchtown. The sprawling plantation had once been a large Scottish settlement. There was a splendid house on the property. Every evening, the family gathered in the living room around the crackling fire in the great fireplace. The Paynes were surrounded by an atmosphere of love and prosperity.

Dolley grew up in the shadow of her two older brothers, Walter and William Temple. She was looked after by Mother Amy, a devoted slave. Ownership of African slaves was legal at the time and commonly practiced in the American colonies. Although Quakers opposed slavery, the existing laws would not allow them to free slaves. As a result, the Paynes, like other slaveholders, benefited from the free labor.

After two years, the family moved to Coles Hill, another plantation close to Scotchtown. Here Dolley tucked away her fondest childhood memories of plantation life, Quaker hospitality, and school days. Eventually, she welcomed into the family five more

ed the meetings and kept all the records. Eventually, they became respected elders, or leaders, in the group. When Dolley's father became a minister, he was allowed to preach.

The Quakers

✷ ✷

The Society of Friends was organized in the 1650s in England. Quakers, as they are called, are against war and believe in the equality of all people. Slavery was especially offensive to them. Punished for their ideas in England, many Quakers fled to the New World. There, William Penn had established Pennsylvania in 1682 as a safe haven for them. Other groups of Quakers lived throughout the colonies. Quakers worship in meetings that begin with silent meditation. Only those moved by the spirit of God speak during the meetings. The name Quaker comes from the trembling that sometimes overcomes someone so moved. More than 300,000 Quakers live around the world today.

An early Philadelphia Quaker meeting

brothers and sisters: Isaac, Lucy, Anna, Mary, and John. Each brought her added responsibilities. As the oldest daughter, Dolley was expected to help watch over them.

The Payne children were raised in the Quaker tradition and attended a Quaker common school. Both boys and girls were taught to read and write from strict Quaker teachings. Only boys learned mathematics, for an additional fee.

According to custom, Quaker children played only with other Quaker children. They were taught to reject worldly pleasures such as dancing,

15

☆ ☆

Dolley Madison was born into a rapidly changing world in 1768. America was still a collection of British colonies, but rebellion stirred everywhere. British taxes on tea and other goods made the colonists so angry that they refused to buy British products.

The colonies bustled with activity. The total population had reached nearly 2 million. Philadelphia was the largest and most modern city. Here were North America's first hospital and medical school, libraries, and newspapers.

Most Americans lived in the countryside, where nearly everything needed for life was grown on the farm or made at home. Fathers and sons worked outdoors. Women and girls labored at "indoor chores." In the South, where Dolley was born, large plantations depended on the labor of African slaves. Beyond the farms and villages lay a vast frontier. Americans eagerly pushed west, even though the king of England had forbidden it.

The disobedience and independent spirit of the colonists alarmed the British. The British king sent more and more troops to keep the peace and control the colonies. The British sang a song called "Yankee Doodle" to make fun of the Americans. Patriots proudly made it an anthem of the cause. By 1768, it was on everyone's lips.

public entertainment, and colorful clothing. The Society of Friends provided their own entertainment.

Quakers dressed in plain clothes made of coarse fabric. Girls and women wore long, gray dresses and bonnets. Lace, colorful fabric, ribbons, and jewelry, which were considered frivolous and vain, were not permitted. Such restrictions were difficult for Dolley. She loved pretty things and cared about her appearance.

For the most part, Quakers kept themselves separated and protected as

The Paynes' Scotchtown estate

much as possible from the outside world. Their belief in truthfulness, hospitality, and brotherly love brought them the respect of their neighbors. Their antislavery, antiwar stand, however, separated them from the rest of society.

During the years the Paynes lived in Virginia, the American colonies declared their independence from England. Eventually, they won their freedom with the Revolution. Living at Coles Hill put the Paynes right in the thick of things. However, like

The American Revolution: Fast Facts

WHAT: The war for American independence

WHEN: 1775–1783

WHO: Between England and the thirteen American colonies. France and Spain joined the war in support of America in 1778.

WHERE: Along the east coast of North America, and as far west as Indiana, with major battles in Massachusetts, New York, New Jersey, Pennsylvania, the Carolinas, Virginia, and Canada.

WHY: Began as a dispute between colonists and king over Britain's authority and its power to tax and control trade in the American colonies. On July 4, 1776, when leading American patriots signed the Declaration of Independence, everything changed. Now, the colonists were fighting for their independence from Britain.

OUTCOME: An American victory at Yorktown, Virginia, ended the fighting, but it took two more years for a treaty to be signed. Finally, in 1783, England recognized the United States of America with the Treaty of Paris.

other Quakers who rejected war, Dolley's family kept themselves apart from the conflict. They did not join the Continental Association that planted the seeds of revolution, and they did not take sides during the war.

Only after the war did the Paynes take sides on an issue very important to them—slavery. In 1782, the Virginia legislature passed a law permitting slaveholders to free slaves. Dolley's parents were among the first Quakers to act on this law. Following their consciences, they freed their slaves and sold their Virginia estate. They moved with their eight children to Philadelphia, the city of Brotherly Love. Mother Amy accompanied them. Now, however, the Paynes were paying her for her services.

✫ ✫ ✫ ✫ ✫ ✫ ✫ ✫ ✫ ✫ ✫ ✫ ✫ ✫ ✫

CHAPTER TWO

A New Beginning

⋆ ⋆ ⋆ ⋆ ⋆ ⋆ ⋆ ⋆ ⋆ ⋆ ⋆ ⋆ ⋆ ⋆ ⋆ ⋆

Dolley was fifteen in 1783 when she arrived in Philadelphia. The family rented a two-story frame house. Mr. Payne set up a small business making and selling laundry starch in the front room down-stairs. Used to more spacious rooms, the family felt squeezed into this new home. The four girls shared one bedroom, while Mother Amy and the boys made do in the attic. Over the next few years, the family lived in several different homes.

In the 1780s, Philadelphia was the largest and most exciting city in the American colonies, and one of its busiest ports. Pennsylvania had been founded on the

⋆ ⋆ ⋆ ⋆ ⋆ ⋆ ⋆ ⋆ ⋆ ⋆ ⋆ ⋆ ⋆ ⋆ ⋆ ⋆

In 1783, the bustling city of Philadelphia had many modern institutions, including a college, a medical school, a theater, and a hospital (above).

principals of religious and economic freedom. It was a haven for people fleeing famine, poverty, and war. It also was the center of American protest against England. During most of the Revolutionary War, Philadelphia was the capital of the American colonies.

At the time the Paynes arrived in the bustling city, the population was nearly 30,000. The city had a college, a medical school, a hospital, a library, a theater, a home for the aged, a prison, a volunteer fire department, and several schools for the education of young ladies.

In the heart of the city stood Philadelphia's finest hotel, the Indian Queen. Stagecoaches arrived there and departed daily, carrying government officials and foreign travelers. Nearby, a huge food market attracted all types of people. The shopping district teemed with dressmakers, milliners, and hairdressers. Throughout the city, the clatter of horses' hooves, the cries of street vendors, and the chimes of church bells could be heard.

Living in Philadelphia opened up a new world for the Payne children. Fifteen-year-old Dolley found the new world particularly exciting. All around her people were making history: Benjamin Franklin, Thomas Jefferson, George Washington, and members of the Continental Congress. They were risking their reputations, and even

Philadelphia's well-stocked High Street food market attracted all types of people.

Dolley Madison was enchanted by the elegantly dressed Philadelphia women she saw in the city's fashionable Chestnut Street shopping district.

their lives, for the freedom and liberty of the new nation. Carpenters' Hall, the State House, and the Liberty Bell would one day become monuments to their sacrifices.

But of all the things that captivated Dolley, what interested her most was the elegant dress and behavior of Philadelphia women. Dolley, like many women of her time, considered Philadelphia fashion the best in the country.

As a typical Quaker young lady, Dolley did not attend formal school. She did continue to receive religious training from her elders and learned the polite art of letter writing. She was allowed to associate freely with other young people at picnics, tea parties, and social events. Always popular,

Fashion Statements

✫ ✫

Most Americans wore very simple clothing. Country families wove their own materials. When King George forbade colonists to weave their own cloth, patriotic women wove it anyway. Their homemade cloth became a symbol of the Revolution. People in the cities, however, could buy elegant European fabrics and accessories. A new dress style inspired by ancient Greece came from France in the

1790s. This style had no fussy petticoats, tall powdered wigs, or expensive fabrics that most wealthy people wore. Instead, women curled their hair and wore high-waisted dresses that flowed freely to the floor. Americans liked this fashion because its simplicity seemed to represent the ideals of the young democracy. Dolley Madison is usually pictured wearing this style.

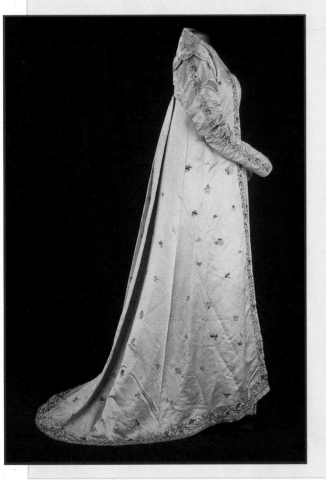

Above: An example of Philadelphia fashion that was popular when Dolley arrived in the city

Left: One of Dolley Madison's embroidered gowns in the French style inspired by ancient Greece

Dolley had several girlfriends and many interested male suitors. But she was not quite ready to settle down and marry. She kept all her suitors at a comfortable distance, even one particular young man who publicly showed his devotion to her.

Dolley met John Todd, Jr., in 1786. A law student at the time, John was from a well-educated and well-respected Quaker family. He refused to be discouraged by Dolley's disinterest in marriage and continued to court her.

When the Payne family arrived in Philadelphia, the Quaker community warmly welcomed them into the Pine Street Monthly Meeting. They also joyfully witnessed the birth of the

Dolley did not attend formal school in Philadelphia, but she continued to receive religious training from her elders.

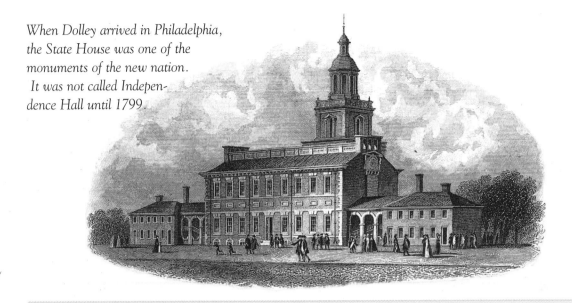

When Dolley arrived in Philadelphia, the State House was one of the monuments of the new nation. It was not called Independence Hall until 1799.

Growing Up in Young America

★ ★ ★ ★ ★ ★ ★ ★ ★ ★ ★ ★ ★ ★ ★ ★ ★ ★ ★ ★

In many ways, young Americans of Dolley Madison's generation grew up fast. Life could be difficult and sometimes short. Many children died in infancy. People of the time did not know how to treat many illnesses. On the farms, even very young children helped tend fields and animals. Mothers taught their daughters to weave, sew, and keep house. Most girls married in their twenties. Boys served in the militia beginning at age sixteen. Drummer boys might be as young as ten. Both boys and girls wore "frocks," or loose-fitting gowns, until they were about six. After that, children dressed as adults did.

Colonial children were not required to attend school. Education was a luxury, especially since there was so much work to be done at home. On Southern plantations, it was illegal to teach slaves to read or to write. As a result, most Americans could neither read nor write. After the Revolution, however, Americans began to realize that educated people were needed to build a strong country. Public school systems took shape. In Massachusetts, laws even required schools to be open to girls. A revolutionary idea indeed!

The Philadelphia Library (above) has used this request box (inset) since the library was founded.

Payne's ninth child—a baby girl named Philadelphia. With the birth of this new baby, the Paynes believed their lives were blessed. Unfortunately, Philadelphia died in infancy. Her death was the first of a long line of tragedies to befall them.

In 1785, Dolley's oldest brother, Walter, sailed to England and was never heard from again. Then, Mr.

Let Freedom Ring

⋆ ⋆

The bell now known as the Liberty Bell was made long before the American Revolution. It was first known as the Old State House Bell. When it rang to announce the adoption of the Declaration of Independence in 1776, it became a symbol of American independence. The bell hung in Philadelphia's Independence Hall and was rung every year on July 4 until 1835. Then, a crack began to widen. It was no longer safe to ring the bell. The Liberty Bell remains a powerful symbol of American ideals. Its inscription reads: "Proclaim liberty throughout all the land unto all the inhabitants thereof."

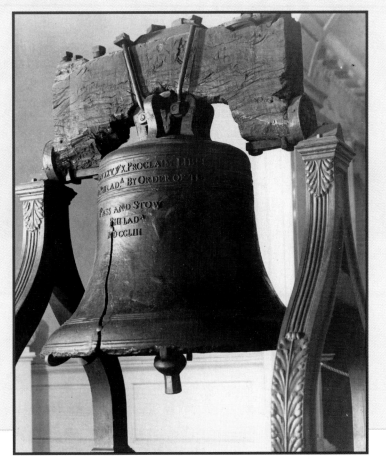

As a center of the Quaker faith, Philadelphia boasted many Quaker meetinghouses, including this one at Fourth and Arch streets.

Payne's business failed. When he finally declared bankruptcy in 1789, the Pine Street Meeting publicly disowned him for not paying his debts. Feeling disgraced, Mr. Payne refused to be seen in public and became a recluse in his own home.

To generate income, Mrs. Payne began taking in boarders. During these trying times, Dolley accepted John Todd's proposal of marriage. Under his loving care, she knew that her mother would have one less child to worry about. And she was right.

After Mr. Payne's business failed, Dolley's mother began taking in boarders at 150 North Third Street.

✯ ✯ ✯ ✯ ✯ ✯ ✯ ✯ ✯ ✯ ✯ ✯ ✯ ✯

CHAPTER THREE

Devoted Wife and Mother

☆ ☆ ☆ ☆ ☆ ☆ ☆ ☆ ☆ ☆ ☆ ☆ ☆ ☆ ☆ ☆

On January 7, 1790, twenty-two-year-old Dolley and twenty-seven-year-old John Todd were married at the Pine Street Meeting House. According to traditional Quaker custom, no elder or minister was present at their wedding, only family and friends. With their parents' consent, and in front of eighty wedding guests, the young couple pledged their affection and loyalty to each other and signed an official marriage certificate. Each of their guests signed it, too.

Elsewhere, the city buzzed with excitement. Buildings were being prepared for the return of Congress from New York City. During the Revolution, Congress

☆ ☆ ☆ ☆ ☆ ☆ ☆ ☆ ☆ ☆ ☆ ☆ ☆ ☆ ☆ ☆

The interior of the Pine Street Meeting House, where Dolley Payne and John Todd were married on January 7, 1790

George Washington (1732–1799)

✮ ✮

So familiar are George Washington's name and face, we forget that they belong to a real person. Washington joined the colonial army at the age of twenty and by the age of twenty-three was a colonel. The tall Virginian retired in 1758 and went home to his beloved estate at Mount Vernon. From there, he took up the cause of independence. As commander of the Continental army and in two terms as the nation's first president, Washington guided the country from colony to democracy. With no presidents before him, Washington knew that he would set the tone for governing the new nation. His intelligence and sound judgment won him the admiration of his troops, the respect of his colleagues, and a place in history.

had moved around to avoid the British. In 1784, New York City became the first capital of the new nation. Congress remained there until the Constitution was approved in 1788. George Washington, the first president, was inaugurated in New York the following year. Congress returned to Philadelphia in 1790 to take up residence in the city's new County Court House. Ten years later, the government would move to Washington, D.C. Newly elected President George Washington was looking for a house in the city. The ever-popular Indian Queen was being spruced up, and some private homes were advertising rooms for rent.

Ignoring all the activity, John and Dolley moved into a small house on Chestnut Street. John set up his law office in the front room on the first floor. Dolley prepared her home in the style of Quaker custom and hospitality. With the return of Congress, John's business prospered. Within two years, he and Dolley had enough money to buy a large home with an attached stable on the corner of Fourth and Walnut streets.

Independence Square was a center of activity, especially during the years between 1790 and 1800, when Philadelphia was the nation's capital.

Among the pieces of fine furniture purchased by Dolley for her large new home were Windsor armchairs like this one.

Now for the first time, Dolley could furnish a home as she wished. She bought fine furniture of mahogany and pine. She purchased Franklin stoves, Windsor chairs, and elaborate tables. She even bought a wooden and glass cupboard to display fine china and silver.

At the time they moved to Fourth Street, Dolley was expecting her first child. She gave birth to a boy on February 29, 1792. Dolley and John named him John Payne. They called

The Todds' Philadelphia home at the corner of Fourth and Walnut streets

The American Plague

★ ★

Early Americans dreaded the disease known as yellow fever, or "Yellow Jack." Originally found in the tropics, it came to America through the slave trade. Caused by a deadly virus, the disease turns the skin yellow and causes a high fever. Before doctors knew how to stop it, yellow fever spread easily. During the 1793 outbreak in Philadelphia, 5,000 people died. Because no one understood that only mosquitoes carry the virus, people avoided contact with one another during epidemics. They believed they might catch yellow fever through a handshake or from the air; they did not suspect a mosquito bite. Today, the disease is kept in check through vaccination and mosquito control.

him Payne. Dolley was content with her life and expected to enjoy a long, happy, and uneventful marriage. However, a series of tragic events occurred over the next two years that changed the couple's lives forever.

In October, Dolley's father died. A short time later, Mother Amy, Dolley's childhood nanny, also passed away. Then, Dolley's fifteen-year-old sister Lucy eloped. She married seventeen-year-old George Steptoe Washington, nephew of President George Washington. Even though the marriage was to the respected Washington family, Dolley and her mother disapproved of it. The groom was not a Quaker. After her marriage, Lucy was banished from Quaker society.

In September of 1793, Dolley gave

birth to her second child, also a boy. He was named William Temple in honor of Dolley's brother. At the time, a yellow fever epidemic was spreading through Philadelphia. To keep Dolley and the boys safe, John took them to Gray's Ferry. Once a pleasure resort, it was now a refuge for frightened Philadelphians waiting for the deadly epidemic to run its course.

John left Dolley with her family and returned to Philadelphia to care for his parents and friends. He assisted with deaths, funerals, and the preparation of wills until his own parents died in October. John remained in the city until October 24. Then, after feeling sickly himself, he went to be with Dolley and the boys. He died only a few hours after he arrived. Baby William died the same day.

Overcome with grief, Dolley fell ill. For several weeks, her condition worsened. Under her mother's loving care, she recovered. Somehow, she found the strength to rise above her losses. She was finally able to accept the fact that her father, her husband, her baby son, and her in-laws had died in the span of only a year.

In November, after the epidemic had ended, Dolley and her mother returned to Philadelphia. Both widows now, they relied on each other for comfort. Immediately, Lucy and young George Steptoe Washington—who only a year earlier had been disowned by the Payne family—asked Lucy's mother to live with them at the Harewood estate in Virginia. Mrs. Payne accepted their invitation and went to Harewood with her daughter Mary and youngest son, John.

Dolley remained in Philadelphia, alone for the first time in her life. At the age of twenty-five, she was determined to live independently. She opened her house on Fourth Street and became the sole guardian of her young son Payne and thirteen-year-old sister Anna. With the comfortable amount of money and property that her husband had left her, Dolley began her new life in earnest.

That winter, in the absence of family, she renewed earlier friendships. By springtime, Dolley's reputation as a beautiful, self-assured widow began attracting suitors. In those days, widows were not expected to mourn for long.

Daughters of Liberty

✮ ✮

Throughout her lifetime, Dolley Madison witnessed many changes in the lives of American women. Not all of them were positive. The American Revolution gave American women some new opportunities. Until the war, wives, mothers, and daughters lived under the control of the men in their lives. Women concerned themselves mostly with life in the home. As war became more certain, however, the "Daughters of Liberty" discovered that they had more power than they thought. They boycotted British products and defied British laws. Those acts helped to stir up the rebellion and raise patriotic spirits. The women burned British goods in huge bonfires to protest unfair taxes. As their husbands, sons, and fathers left for the battlefield, women had new responsibilities. They found themselves managing farms and businesses with increasing confidence and skill. Some even enlisted in the army. The Revolution gave women some independence.

Under the laws of the new country, however, women had no rights. They could not vote, own property, hold public office, or attend college. Husbands "owned" their wives. Wives owned nothing, not even their clothes. Women of the Revolution, who had tasted independence, protested. But it made no difference. Women's roles became strictly defined and limited to the household.

It would not be enough. In 1848, the year before Dolley's death, a group of women gathered in Seneca Falls, New York. Inspired by the growing movement to abolish slavery, they believed in equal rights for women under the law. Using the powerful language of the Declaration of Independence, they drafted a manifesto of women's rights. It was called the Declaration of Sentiments. What Dolley Madison's patriotic generation had begun, these women would continue. They launched the first organized women's movement.

CHAPTER FOUR

Starting Over

* * * * * * * * * * * * * * * * *

Less than a year after her husband's death, Dolley met James Madison. Aaron Burr, a mutual friend, introduced Dolley and James in the spring of 1794. Madison was called "Jemmy" by his close friends and the "Great Little Madison" by others. He was a forty-three-year-old congressman from Virginia who was seventeen years older than Dolley. At only five feet six inches tall, he was about the same height as Dolley. James came from a wealthy, educated Virginia family and was a brilliant scholar and writer.

James Madison had been an American patriot from 1772 until the colonies won their independence in

* * * * * * * * * * * * * * * * *

The first Continental Congress met in Carpenters' Hall (right); the second met in the State House, later called Independence Hall.

1783. He served in Virginia's first legislative assembly in 1776 and was Virginia's delegate to the Continental Congress in 1779. He was a member of Congress from 1780 to 1783. Madison was Virginia's delegate to the Constitutional Convention in Philadelphia in 1787. As such, he participated in writing the U.S. Constitution and persuading eleven of the thirteen states to ratify, or approve, it. Later, he was largely responsible for drafting the first ten amendments to the Constitution (the Bill of Rights). In 1789, James Madison and Thomas Jefferson organized the Democratic-Republican

The Road to Union

★ ★

After the Revolution, the hard work began. Americans had won their independence from Britain. Now they would have to form a new government to replace British rule. That overwhelming task did not go smoothly. No one could agree on the terms that would unite the states. Each state, in fact, considered itself an independent nation. Imagine the confusion in 1787 when leaders called a convention in Philadelphia to tackle the issues. Should there be a strong central government? Should the states be independent? Should America be a patchwork of countries or come together under one leader? Finally, after a hot summer of debate and compromise, delegates crafted the Constitution. It contains laws for governing the country and describes how the government should be set up. It still guides us today and is the oldest national constitution in effect in the world.

Washington addresses the 1787 Constitutional Convention.

It took nearly a year for enough states to approve the Constitution and agree to become the United States. However, many people were concerned over the dangers of a powerful central government. They feared that the rights of individuals had not been guaranteed in this important document. Using the suggestions of several states, James Madison drew up a list of ten basic rights to which all Americans would be entitled. They include freedom of religion, of speech, and of the press. These first ten amendments, or additions, to the Constitution are known as the Bill of Rights. They became part of the Constitution in 1791.

Party, which later became today's Democratic Party.

After Madison's first formal meeting with Dolley, he lost no time in making clear his intentions to marry her. For several weeks, they corresponded with each other. A proposal of marriage followed. Immediately, Madison's interest in Dolley became public and rumors began to fly. When Martha and George Washington heard the news, they encouraged Dolley to accept the proposal.

To slow down the speed of events and give herself time to think, Dolley decided to go away for the summer. Packing her things, she took Payne and Anna to visit her great-uncle in Virginia. Madison also left Philadelphia on congressional vacation. He returned to Montpelier and anxiously waited to hear from Dolley.

In August, Dolley left her uncle's estate and headed for Harewood to visit her sister. On the way, she stopped at Fredericksburg to change stagecoaches. There, she hastily wrote two letters—one to Mr. Madison, accepting his marriage proposal, and the other to her lawyer in Philadelphia. Dolley's decision to remarry had come less than a year after her first husband had died. Although James Madison was seventeen years older than Dolley, and marrying him would mean being disowned by the Quakers, Dolley believed that she was doing the right thing. She proceeded to Harewood, where Madison soon joined her.

Dolley Payne Todd and James

A young James Madison

Martha Washington (1731–1802)

★ ★ ★ ★ ★ ★ ★ ★ ★ ★ ★ ★ ★ ★ ★ ★ ★ ★ ★ ★

A young widow with two children, Martha Dandridge Custis married George Washington in 1759. For sixteen years, she supervised the bustling household at Mount Vernon, even during the sad time after the death of her beloved daughter in 1773. During the Revolution, Martha often visited her husband's field headquarters, bringing reminders of home to Washington and his men. As the first First Lady, Martha had no role models. Even though America was a democracy, some people wanted to call her "Lady Washington," as if she were royalty. A gracious hostess, Martha Washington set the example for First Ladies to come.

Dolley Payne Todd and James Madison were married at Harewood (above), the estate owned by her brother-in-law, George Steptoe Washington.

Madison were married in a quiet ceremony on September 15, 1794. Dolley's mother and sisters, the young George Steptoe Washington household, and a few neighbors were present. An Episcopal clergyman and one of Madison's friends performed the simple ceremony. A high-spirited Virginia celebration followed.

On Dolley's wedding night, she wrote to a friend, "I give my hand to the man who of all others I most admire. . . . In this union, I have everything that is soothing and grateful in prospect . . . and my little Payne will have a generous and tender protector."

A few weeks after the wedding,

Dolley learned what was expected of her as a politician's wife. Because James was needed in Congress, the newlyweds had to drop their plans for Dolley to meet the Madison family at Montpelier. Instead, they returned to Philadelphia early in October. They traveled by way of Harpers Ferry, the shortest but roughest route, and arrived in a broken carriage.

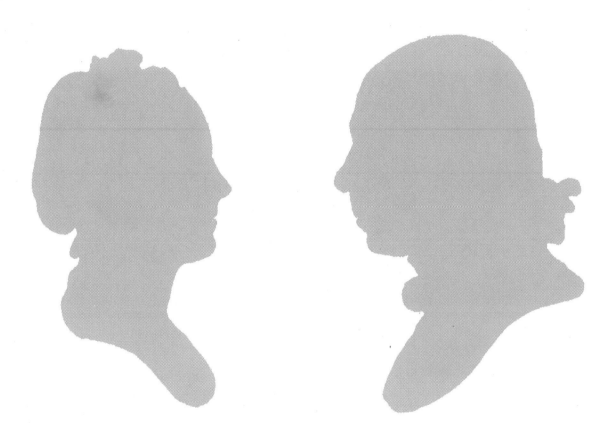

Silhouettes of Dolley and James Madison

CHAPTER FIVE

First Lady of Charm

W hen the Madisons arrived in Philadelphia, they needed a place to live. Dolley had rented out the house that she and John Todd owned. James and Dolley moved temporarily into a house recently left vacant by James Monroe. While James Madison dealt with the urgent business of Congress, Dolley quietly began building a solid network of friends and associates. Although Quaker society had disowned her for marrying a non-Quaker, Dolley did not seem greatly disturbed by it. She enjoyed the elegance and fashion of Philadelphia society. With a rare combination of simple Quaker values and regal conduct, Dolley blossomed in this new environment. She thoroughly enjoyed her new life.

After that first winter, the Madisons moved into a three-story brick house at 4295 Spruce Street. During sessions of Congress, the home was always open. Political friends and foes alike were welcome. In fact, Dolley made sure that every Madison gathering included both Federalists and members of the Republican Party. Among their frequent visitors were President and Mrs. Washington, as well as Republican Thomas Jefferson and Federalist John Adams.

Republican Thomas Jefferson frequently visited the Madison home on Spruce Street.

The First Political Parties

✮ ✮

The authors of the Constitution didn't encourage them, but political parties began to form shortly after independence. Each party supported different ideas about the new government. By 1796, two philosophies had emerged. The Federalists, including George Washington and John Adams, believed in a strong central government and encouraged commerce and growth. The Democratic-Republicans, commonly called the Republicans, were led by James Madison and Thomas Jefferson. The members of that party were more concerned about individual liberties. They believed there should be less governmental control in people's lives. Generally, Federalism was popular in New England and in the cities; in the more rural South, Democratic-Republican ideas appealed.

Even for Dolley, it was not easy to keep a pleasant atmosphere during dinners and receptions attended by political enemies. She worked hard at it. Whenever it appeared that an argument was about to begin, Dolley guided the conversation to other topics. Even though Dolley's social responsibilities were very important to her, she never lost sight of family affairs.

Dolley balanced her public and private life well. She always stayed in touch with her brothers and sisters. She introduced her sister Anna into Philadelphia society. She brought her youngest sister Mary up from the country on frequent visits. Her brothers did not fare as well. In 1795, Temple and Isaac were tragically shot to death in separate incidents.

When James Madison's term in Congress ended in 1797, he and Dolley left Philadelphia. They retired to their Montpelier estate in Orange County, Virginia. The couple planned to enjoy some much-needed rest. The Madisons' retreat from public life did not bring them the rest they needed, however. Dolley totally immersed herself in the task of running a two-family household. Her mother-in-law Nellie became a good friend. Dolley surpassed everyone's expectations as mistress of the plantation.

James's isolation from politics never happened. He remained in daily contact with Vice President Thomas Jefferson. Jefferson strongly opposed the Federalist policies of President John Adams. As Republicans, Madison and Jefferson disagreed with laws

Even though his political views differed from Madison's, John Adams (above) was another frequent visitor to the Madison home.

the Federalists were passing. Those laws strengthened the federal government, threatened the rights of states and citizens, and encouraged war with France. Madison and Jefferson kept busy sponsoring resolutions declaring many of the Federalist laws unconstitutional. Then, from 1799 to 1800, Madison served in the Virginia legislature. There, he led a fight against what he felt were the government's efforts to undermine people's human rights.

When Thomas Jefferson was elected president of the United States in 1800, he appointed Madison secretary of state. Jefferson was a widower who had two daughters. Neither of his daughters was able to serve as his hostess. He asked Mrs. Madison to be his official hostess.

Dolley and James retired to their Montpelier estate in Orange County, Virginia (above), in 1797.

Thomas Jefferson and James Madison discussing the new capital, Washington, D.C.

At thirty-three, Dolley was a perfect choice for the role of substitute First Lady. Because of her seven years of experience as hostess to Philadelphia politicians, Dolley was certainly qualified for the position. She accepted Jefferson's request. From then on, at every presidential dinner or reception, Dolley Madison acted as the official hostess.

The Madisons arrived in Washington, D.C., in May 1801, just as the new capital city was being built. Jemmy, Dolley, nine-year-old Payne, and Anna temporarily moved into the President's House (later called the White House). Permanent quarters were chosen three months later.

The social life of Washington, D.C., was pretty dismal. As the city

Abigail Adams (1744–1818)

★ ★ ★ ★ ★ ★ ★ ★ ★ ★ ★ ★ ★ ★ ★ ★ ★ ★ ★

We know Abigail Adams well because she wrote hundreds of letters throughout her lifetime. Quick-witted and capable, she had strong opinions about equality for women and African-Americans. "Remember the Ladies," she suggested to her husband John Adams in 1776. " [We] will not hold ourselves bound by any Laws in which we have no voice. . . ." Indeed, critics accused her of having too much influence over her husband, who became America's second president in 1797. The Adamses were the first to live in the uncomfortable and incomplete President's House in Washington. There, Abigail hung her clothes to dry in one of the huge, unfinished rooms.

A view of Washington, D.C., as it looked in 1800, just before James and Dolley arrived

After the Madisons moved to Washington, D.C., Dolley's son Payne (above) enrolled at Bishop Carroll's school in Baltimore.

was being built, few homes were suitable for official entertaining. Most politicians and their families looked to the President's House for guidance in matters of social etiquette. As hostess, Dolley drew from the examples of previous First Ladies Martha Washington and Abigail Adams. Eventually, however, she developed a style all her own—one that made her a legend.

At dinners and receptions, Dolley dressed ornately and colorfully. White was reserved for state occasions. She ordered all her gowns from France. They were very expensive. Dolley always wore matching accessories—gloves, slippers, jewelry, and feathered turbans, which became her trademark. In time, Dolley became the undisputed fashion leader in Washington.

During the years Dolley served as Jefferson's official hostess, great changes occurred in her family. Her sister Anna married Congressman Richard Cutts and left the Madison household. Payne enrolled at Bishop John Carroll's school in Baltimore. Both her mother and her sister Mary died. Each of these events took away the companionship of those she loved. Each also brought her closer to her destiny as First Lady and wife of the president of the United States.

✦ ✦ ✦ ✦ ✦ ✦ ✦ ✦ ✦ ✦ ✦ ✦ ✦ ✦ ✦

CHAPTER SIX

Washington's Finest Hostess

✴ ✴ ✴ ✴ ✴ ✴ ✴ ✴ ✴ ✴ ✴ ✴ ✴ ✴ ✴ ✴

Thomas Jefferson had groomed the Madisons to replace him in the President's House after his term ended. He was confident that the policies he and Madison had begun would continue. As expected, when James officially took office, he was well prepared for the job. And so was Dolley.

The new First Lady moved into the President's House on March 4, 1809, at the peak of her social success. James had to deal with the growing problems of trade and threats of war with England. Dolley had to figure out how to furnish the President's House. When Jefferson was president, outside terraces and landscap-

✴ ✴ ✴ ✴ ✴ ✴ ✴ ✴ ✴ ✴ ✴ ✴ ✴ ✴ ✴ ✴

A view of the President's House (now the White House) as it looked in 1809, when the Madisons moved in

ing had been completed. But little effort had been made to furnish the inside of the house. Jefferson had used his own furniture from Monticello to help fill the large house.

Congress allocated thousands of dollars to furnish the President's House. Benjamin Latrobe was hired to handle the decorating, but Dolley's taste and good judgment were needed. Although none of her original fur-

nishings remain, written accounts describe them as elegant and cheerful. Gorgeous mirrors reflected and expanded the great chambers. Elaborate mantelpieces were installed. Handsome oil lamps provided soft, glowing light. A piano and guitar added color and music to the environment. By August, the work was nearly complete.

Dolley's schedule as First Lady was

58

Benjamin Latrobe (1764–1820)

★ ★ ★ ★ ★ ★ ★ ★ ★ ★ ★ ★ ★ ★ ★ ★

Although he was born in England, Latrobe became early America's most famous architect after coming here in 1796. He admired ancient Greek architecture and made the Greek style popular in the United States, especially for banks, government buildings, and universities. President Jefferson hired him to work on the Capitol in Washington, D.C., in 1803. Since the outside had already been designed, Latrobe worked on the interior. There, he topped off Greek-style columns with corn and tobacco designs, symbols of American agriculture. After the British burned the Capitol in the War of 1812, Latrobe helped to rebuild it.

The President's House East Room as designed by Benjamin Latrobe

This dinner plate was part of the Madison's official President's House china set.

A view of the State Dining Room as it looked with Latrobe's designs

Benjamin Latrobe designed Greek-style chairs like this one for the President's House dining room.

busy. Every day, until about three o'clock or so, she carried on her daily rounds of housekeeping and received visitors. By four o'clock, the usual dinner hour in Washington, Dolley had changed from her Quaker gray dress, with white apron and white kerchief, to a dress in the latest color and style of European fashion.

At all formal dinner parties, Dolley presided at the head of the table. Guests sat on her left and right. The president sat comfortably on the side. This custom, which was the president's idea, relieved him of having to lead the conversation. Dolley had fine-tuned her social skills over the years and was a better conversationalist.

After dinner, guests retired to the drawing room. There they continued to engage in

During the time Madison held office, the President's House was the center of social activity.

61

What's for Dinner?

✳ ✳

George Washington loved ice cream—he spent $200 on it during the summer of 1790. Thomas Jefferson was a gourmet who delighted in giving parties. Most Americans loved to eat, and the bounty of the land obliged their hearty appetites. They preferred plain food: oysters, pork, puddings, and bread were particularly popular.

But Americans didn't particularly like vegetables, and they believed that fresh fruits caused diseases. Surprised foreign visitors described a nation constantly eating and suffering from indigestion. In well-to-do homes, fancy dinner parties might last hours, as guests lingered around beautiful tables set with sparkling crystal, china, and silverware. French cooking was fashionable for such events. Dolley Madison's favorite dish was called *pot-au-feu*, a soup of vegetables and meat, which she often served as Jefferson's hostess. She is also remembered for another delicacy, as this White House guest recalled: "Mrs. Madison always entertains with Grace and Charm, but last night there was a sparkle in her eye that set astir an Air of Expectancy among her Guests. When finally the brilliant Assemblage—America's best— entered the dining room, they beheld a Table set with French china and English silver, laden with good things to eat, and in the Centre high on a silver platter, a large, shining dome of pink Ice Cream."

An Old New American Style

✶ ✶

To honor their new country, Americans adopted a new style of architecture. But it was based on a very old style that the ancient Greeks and Romans had used. Thomas Jefferson (himself an amateur architect) thought that the balance, dignity, and simplicity of ancient Roman buildings perfectly expressed America's democratic ideals. Unlike royal palaces, they were not showy or ornate. Furniture, too, became simple and elegant. For decoration, Americans added their own symbols of the young country to these antique forms. Eagles were especially popular and appeared everywhere—from mirrors to bars of soap. Many people feel that this neoclassical (new-classical) style was the first that was truly American. Therefore, it is often called Federal style.

lively conversation. Dolley always entered the drawing room with a book in her hand, as she said ". . . to have something not ungraceful to say, and if need be, to supply a word of talk."

On Wednesday nights, receptions were open to everyone. No invitations were required. Congressmen, diplomats, government officials, and foreign dignitaries came. Curious out-of-town visitors and townspeople looking for gossip and the latest fashions joined the gathering, too. No matter what their position, everyone was treated with interest and respect.

In public, Dolley never commented on political issues. She also refrained from common gossip. "It is one of my sources of happiness," she often told others, "never to desire a knowledge of other people's business." This admirable quality drew people to her. While Madison was in office, the President's House was the center of all activity in Washington and Dolley was the most popular person in it.

✶ ✶ ✶ ✶ ✶ ✶ ✶ ✶ ✶ ✶ ✶ ✶ ✶ ✶ ✶

CHAPTER SEVEN

Partners in Politics and War

✯ ✯ ✯ ✯ ✯ ✯ ✯ ✯ ✯ ✯ ✯ ✯ ✯ ✯ ✯ ✯

Dolley's popularity with the American people
played a major role in her husband's winning a
second term as president in 1812. Before the election,
however, the president's popularity had begun to
decline. The British were blocking American ships
from trading in European ports—and Madison hadn't
been able to do anything about it. The British were
also taking American sailors from their ships and
impressing them into the British navy. To make matters worse, the British were arming Native Americans
in the Northwest Territory. They were trying to keep
the United States from expanding its borders.

✯ ✯ ✯ ✯ ✯ ✯ ✯ ✯ ✯ ✯ ✯ ✯ ✯ ✯ ✯ ✯

The president asked Congress to declare war against England. On June 18, 1812, Congress did so. Madison's Federalist enemies called it "Mr. Madison's War." Although unprepared for war, the United States began fighting the British—on land and on sea. Fighting broke out first along the Great Lakes and the Canadian border. There, the British navy and British fortresses blocked a U.S. invasion. The British also blockaded the Atlantic coast. They planned to crush the U.S. Navy and invade the United States.

While the war raged in such places as Lake Erie and Lake Champlain, Dolley continued her normal round of social events and entertaining in Washington. She was less carefree than usual, however. As the first year of war dragged on into the next, it began taking its toll on the Madisons. In June 1813, the president fell ill with a terrible fever. He was near death for several weeks. Dolley paid no attention to the recent threats of a British invasion of Washington. She stayed to nurse the president back to health. Bravely, she handled the situation alone. Her son Payne, who might

have been some comfort, was in Europe.

Another year passed and still the war dragged on. By 1814, however, it was clear that the British would probably win. On August 18, Americans' fears of an invasion came true. Nearly 5,000 British troops began to march on the city.

After hearing of the invasion, President Madison joined General Winder and the troops that were preparing to defend the city. He asked Dolley to remain at the President's House until he returned. He thought he would be back by August 23 or 24. On Tuesday, August 22, only Dolley and a small group of frightened servants were at the President's House. Her husband sent word that the number of British troops was much larger than they had thought. He told Dolley to be ready to leave the city at a moment's notice because the enemy might be coming to destroy it.

Needing to communicate with someone about her desperate situation, Dolley began a letter to her sister Lucy. For all she knew at the time, it might be her last. In the letter, Dolley

U.S. naval forces commanded by Thomas Macdonough were victors over the British in the 1814 Battle of Lake Champlain.

explains how she packed important "Cabinet Papers" into trunks, loaded a wagon with as many valuable articles as it would hold, and anxiously waited for her husband to return.

On August 24, the British marched toward the capital. They easily swept over the small contingent of inexperienced troops who guarded the road at Bladensburg. That morning, Dolley added another entry to her sister's letter. She mentioned the sound of cannon coming from the direction of Bladensburg. "Since sunrise," she wrote, "I have been turning my spyglass in every direction and watching with unwearied anxiety, hoping to discern the approach of my dear husband and his friends; but, alas, I can descry only groups of military wandering in all directions, as if there was a lack of arms or of spirit to fight for their own firesides! . . . "

By three o'clock or so, Dolley knew she should wait no longer. She did insist on adding an important portrait of George Washington to her store of things for safekeeping. As she wrote to her sister, "Our kind friend, Mr. Carrol, has come to hasten my departure, and

First Lady Dolley Madison

is in a very bad humor with me because I insist on waiting until the large picture of Gen. Washington is secured, and it requires to be unscrewed from the wall. This process was found too tedious for these perilous moments; I have ordered the frame to be broken and the canvas taken out; it is done—and the precious portrait placed in the hands of two gentlemen of New York for safe keeping."

With her maid Sukey and another servant, she joined the rest of the

The Declaration of Independence was one of the most important documents saved by Dolley Madison as the British were invading the capital.

A Familiar Face

* *

The portrait that Dolley Madison rescued from the President's House is today the most familiar image we have of George Washington. Since well before the Revolution, American artists loved to paint portraits. Gilbert Stuart became famous painting portraits of Washington, of whom he made at least 114. All of them were based on three he did from life in 1795 and 1796. Stuart painted this version in 1797. Today, it hangs in the East Room of the White House, thanks to Dolley Madison. President Washington's peculiar facial expression may have been caused by an ill-fitting set of false teeth.

The President's House and many other government buildings were set ablaze during the British attack on Washington, D.C.

army of Washington citizens rushing from the capital that afternoon. Only minutes later, Madison and a few companions returned to the abandoned house. But with the British close behind, they quickly rode on.

Dolley Madison was safely out of the city by evening when the British arrived. She had left nothing of political importance in the President's House for the enemy to destroy. Important "Cabinet Papers" and national keepsakes had been saved.

The British set fire to the Capitol. They completely destroyed the House of Representatives and damaged the

The War of 1812: Fast Facts

WHAT: "Second War of American Independence"

WHEN: 1812-1815

WHO: Between Britain and the United States

WHERE: Battles took place from Canada south to New Orleans, and as far west as the Great Lakes, with many important naval engagements

The Battle of Lake Erie, September 1813

WHY: Britain and France, who were at war with each other, were keeping the United States from trading freely, putting the new country's economy in danger. Other issues involved the British practices of impressing American sailors for British service and arming Native Americans in the Northwest Territory.

OUTCOME: Little was gained by either side, and there was much loss of life. However, the United States emerged with a new sense of nationhood and national pride.

Senate. They left the President's House blazing in the night sky as they ransacked the city and terrorized its people.

Late afternoon of the following day, Dolley met Jemmy in secret. They arrived just as a thunderstorm broke. The roaring winds and sheets of rain put out the fires still smoldering in the capital. After the storm began to lessen, the British troops left. They thought the storm was an omen, and feared that the Americans might cut off their retreat to Chesapeake Bay.

On Friday morning, the president went to join American troops re-organizing north of Washington. Dolley left the wagon containing the president's things with Sukey. She went on with two armed male companions. Dressed as farmers, the three moved about for the next few days unrecognized.

While British troops had been burning and plundering Washington,

Dolley Madison, along with huge crowds of other citizens, fled the capital during the British invasion.

The Octagon

☆ ☆

This unusual brick residence, built about 1800, occupies an oddly shaped lot near the White House. One of Washington's oldest houses, it escaped British torches during the War of 1812. The owners had fled to their country estate before the invasion. They offered the home to the Madisons when the smoke cleared. Five months after they moved in, President Madison signed the Treaty of Ghent there to end the war. Dolley's lively parties filled the house with politicians, diplomats, and members of Washington society. Local legend suggests that Dolley's spirit still haunts the Octagon.

The elegant staircase in the Octagon

The exterior of the Octagon, or Tayloe House

A view of the President's House, later called the White House, after the fire of 1814

troops from British ships on the Potomac River were robbing Alexandria's warehouses. Their looting and destruction lasted twelve days. The burning of Washington marked the beginning of the end of the war. However, a second British invasion through Florida had begun. Secretary of War James Monroe ordered General Andrew Jackson and his vol-

unteer Tennessee army to fight the British in the South.

Shortly after returning to Washington, the Madisons leased the Tayloe House (also called the Octagon). It was the most elegant dwelling still intact after the fire. Immediately, the overwhelming task of rebuilding the city began. Briefly, the government considered relocating the capital

General Andrew Jackson and his Tennessee Volunteers won the Battle of New Orleans on January 8, 1815.

to Philadelphia. The Madisons, however, insisted that the capital should remain in Washington, where the Founding Fathers had meant it to be. Allowing no time to mourn their losses, they called on architect Benjamin Latrobe. They wanted him to restore —and enlarge—the capital's buildings and the President's House. By December, the restoration of Washington was well underway.

On February 4, 1815, news came that General Jackson's forces had defeated the British at New Orleans and the British were retreating. Even greater news followed. On February

President Madison signed the Treaty of Ghent in this room at the Octagon.

14, the U.S. Peace Commission returned to Washington from France with the Treaty of Ghent. This was the official announcement that the War of 1812 was over. Nationwide celebrations followed. For the Madisons, there were several reasons to celebrate. Not only was the war over, but their son also was home and their term in office was coming to an end.

★ ★ ★ ★ ★ ★ ★ ★ ★ ★ ★ ★ ★ ★ ★

CHAPTER EIGHT

The Montpelier Years

* * * * * * * * * * * * * * * * *

Shortly after the war ended, the Madisons' popularity increased. The next two years flew by. They were much less eventful than the previous six years had been. Dolley and James looked forward to retiring to Montpelier. After sixteen years as Washington's First Lady, Dolley was ready to pass on the responsibility to someone else. As their last year in office approached, Dolley and James invited Payne to join them at Montpelier. They hoped he would soon marry and settle down as a farmer in the Madison tradition.

On March 4, 1817, the Madisons attended the inauguration of James Monroe and the ball that followed.

* * * * * * * * * * * * * * * * *

James Monroe (1758–1831)

✦ ✦

James Monroe followed Madison as the fifth president of the United States in 1817. He and Madison were friends, even though they did not always agree.

Although he challenged Madison unsuccessfully for the presidency in 1808, Madison chose him as secretary of state, and later as secretary of war. Honest and hard-working, Monroe served two terms in office during the Era of Good Feelings, which was a time of relative calm and prosperity. Monroe was a lieutenant in the Revolutionary War and a delegate to the Continental Congress. He was the last president whose career spanned the birth of the nation. He was also the third president to die on a Fourth of July.

In 1817, James Monroe followed James Madison as president of the United States.

They stayed only long enough to welcome the Monroes into office and bid farewell to the excited crowd. Then they left Washington.

James, now sixty-six, began managing Montpelier. At the time, the estate was about 4,000 acres (1,619 hectares). Dolley managed the household and cared for the beautiful flower garden Jemmy had designed for her. Entertaining still took up the major part of each day. Friends—and even strangers—stopped at Montpelier. Sometimes they stayed for days. Dolley gave many formal dinner parties, usually for political friends. Although the constant stream of guests was often tiring, the Madisons enjoyed the company. They were able to keep up to date on the news, and they loved being part of the lively discussions.

Dolley and James spent part of each day writing letters and organizing the president's historical papers. During his career, James Madison had taken detailed notes of the secret discussions that led to the drafting and adoption of the U.S. Constitution. He

James Madison designed the beautiful Montpelier gardens that gave Dolley so much pleasure.

Secret Sessions

✫ ✫ ✫ ✫ ✫ ✫ ✫ ✫ ✫ ✫ ✫ ✫ ✫ ✫ ✫ ✫ ✫ ✫ ✫ ✫

In the hot summer of 1787, delegates to the Constitutional Convention debated the new government in secret. They wanted the freedom to talk about issues honestly and change their minds if necessary. The delegates worked hard to prevent information from leaking. They posted guards at the doorways and locked the windows despite the heat. Someone accompanied the aged Ben Franklin to dinner each night to make sure he didn't talk absentmindedly in public. Even Thomas Jefferson, who was in Paris, remained in the dark. How did discussions go in those secret sessions? A curious world would have to wait until James Madison's notes were published fifty years later.

believed that the publication of his papers would be an important source of information for history students. He also felt that their sale would provide an income for Dolley after his death. Therefore, James worked tirelessly to complete them.

Dolley was her husband's faithful secretary. She was also a second pair of eyes and hands when his eyesight and rheumatic fingers failed him. She once expressed how seriously she fulfilled

James Madison as he looked at the age of eighty-two, about three years before he died

this task for him. "In fulfillment of his wishes," she said, "I have therefore devoted myself to the object of having prepared for the press the productions of his pen. It will form the surest evidence of his claim to the gratitude of his country and the world. . . . "

Dolley and James received little help from Payne at Montpelier. He was popular in public and often drank and gambled too much. He never remained home for long. Dolley lavished love and money on him, which he took advantage of and squandered every chance he got. James finally stopped giving him money. That only brought Payne closer to ruin, and he publicly embarrassed the family. In 1829 and 1830, Dolley and James had to rescue Payne from prison where he was being held for failing to pay his debts. Afterward, he returned home, but only for a while.

Throughout Madison's twenty-year retirement at Montpelier, Dolley and Jemmy were devoted companions. As Jemmy's health gradually weakened, Dolley spent more time taking care of him. When he died quietly on June 28, 1836, Dolley felt a profound loss.

Dolley wrote this note to President Martin Van Buren to acknowledge his condolence letter on the death of her husband.

Family and friends came to Dolley's assistance and condolence letters poured in from around the world. Congress gave her the highest honor ever given a president's widow. The members voted her a lifetime seat on the floor of the House. Amid all the attention, Dolley could think of only one thing—fulfilling her final promise to Jemmy. She paid her husband's few

James Madison's gravesite at Montpelier

outstanding debts and distributed the gifts he left to family members. Then, she focused all her attention on publishing his papers.

When no New York publisher showed interest in publishing the papers, Dolley turned to the U.S. government. In December, President Andrew Jackson recommended that Congress buy the papers. In April, Congress authorized the sum of $30,000 as payment for the first volume.

Satisfied that she had made a start in realizing her husband's dream, Dolley left Montpelier in the hands of Payne in the fall of 1837. She returned to Washington, the city she loved.

Andrew Jackson (1767–1845)

✮ ✮ ✮ ✮ ✮ ✮ ✮ ✮ ✮ ✮ ✮

Jackson's undistinguished political career took a turn for the better during the War of 1812 with his several stunning victories over the British and their Indian allies. His triumph at the Battle of New Orleans gave the country the hero it desperately needed after an otherwise badly handled war. Jackson's fiery personality and reputation as a frontiersman appealed to many Americans. He ran for the presidency in 1828, building around him a strong Democratic Party dedicated to the common people. Although his two terms in office were often controversial, he viewed the president as the true representative of the American people and worked to strengthen the chief executive's powers.

CHAPTER NINE

A Life All Her Own

☆ ☆ ☆ ☆ ☆ ☆ ☆ ☆ ☆ ☆ ☆ ☆ ☆ ☆ ☆

Dolley was in her mid-sixties when she returned to Washington, D.C. Her niece Anna accompanied her. Dolley had always treated her brother's daughter, Anna Payne, as the daughter she never had. As her companion, Anna now would help make up for the loneliness Dolley still felt after the death of her beloved Jemmy.

Together, Dolley and Anna moved into a house on Lafayette Square, near the President's House. Martin Van Buren, the current president, was the fourth to occupy the mansion since Dolley had served as First Lady. The President's House was now a gleaming white

☆ ☆ ☆ ☆ ☆ ☆ ☆ ☆ ☆ ☆ ☆ ☆ ☆ ☆ ☆

Dolley and her niece, Anna Payne

mansion. It didn't look much like the first graystone house that Dolley and James had occupied before the fire of 1814. Still, it beckoned to Dolley. And Dolley answered, in spite of her age, with great interest and enthusiasm.

Immediately, Dolley renewed old friendships and resumed her ever-popular receptions. She made room in her house for everyone who came to visit her. Often, the same people who called on the president came to visit her in Lafayette Square. Obviously, Washington society had missed Dolley's warm personal style.

During their first two years in

Dolley Madison and Anna Payne lived in this house on Lafayette Square when they moved to Washington.

The White House as it looked when Dolley returned to Washington in 1837

Washington, Dolley and Anna returned to Montpelier for the summers. When they went to the country estate in June 1839, they remained until October 1841. Because money was running low, they were not able to keep up the Washington lifestyle. Dolley thought she could make an income by farming. But Payne had run Montpelier into the ground. This burdened Dolley with additional expenses. Because she was in grave financial difficulty, Dolley tried to sell the second volume of the Madison papers.

Once again, she tried New York publishers. Once again, there was no interest. With no other income, Dolley had to borrow money on her

In 1844, Dolley's financial situation was so desperate that she was forced to sell the Montpelier estate.

Washington home. In spite of the loan, she had to sell 750 acres (304 ha) of the Montpelier estate and rent out the house. In September 1844, Dolley sold the remaining estate. Then she asked Congress to consider buying the remaining Madison papers. On December 17, 1844, the Senate authorized the purchase and publication of the papers. But the House of Representatives failed to act on it.

After the sale of Montpelier, Dolley and her niece also spent their summers in the capital. As unpaid bills stacked up, Dolley's brush with bankruptcy became public news. At the end of 1847, some of Dolley's friends brought the matter of the

Madison papers before Congress again. This time, however, the issue was proposed as a measure of financial relief for Mrs. Madison. The bill passed. On May 20, 1848, Dolley's eightieth birthday, Congress voted in favor of paying $25,000 for the remaining Madison documents. Dolley immediately received $5,000. The rest was kept as a trust fund from which she would draw an annual income. Dolley and her niece could live comfortably on the income from the papers, but the debts her son Payne had accumulated weighed heavily on her. Desperate to help him, Dolley tried every means to satisfy Payne's creditors.

In June 1849, greed and desperation brought Payne to Washington to see his mother. He insisted that she make out a will. In his own handwriting, Payne prepared a will for her, leaving everything to him. Under such pressure, Dolley signed the will. However, shortly after Payne left, Dolley was able to think more clearly. She asked her nephew Madison Cutts to draw up a new will. This document

divided her trust fund of $20,000 equally between her niece Anna and her son. She left ownership of all her other possessions to Payne.

The experience of making out a will and seeing her son in such a worthless state was heartbreaking for Dolley. Once young at heart, she now aged quickly. In July, Dolley became bedridden. She needed help to sign the new will. A few days later, Dolley slipped into a coma. On the morning of July 12, 1849, she died.

News of Dolley Madison's death spread quickly. It was carried in all the major newspapers and traveled over every telegraph wire. For more than thirty years, Dolley had been a vital part of the Washington social scene. Now it was difficult to accept her absence. In tribute to Dolley, Washington gave her a funeral fit for a president. Representatives of every government office attended the elaborate ceremony. Newspaper eulogies honored Dolley. The Washington *Intelligencer* printed the following eulogy: "She continued until within a few weeks, to grace society with her

Profile of America, 1849: Growing Pains

✶ ✶

Born before the creation of the United States, Dolley Madison lived to see the Union grow to thirty states. By the time of her death in 1849, the United States had expanded in many ways, for better and for worse. The United States acquired most of the Southwest after a war with Mexico. Pioneers pushed the frontier to the Pacific Ocean, and a gold strike lured 80,000 miners to California in 1849. A popular book that year was called *The Oregon Trail*, and everyone was singing "Oh, Susanna," Stephen Foster's song about the gold rush. The fever to expand infected every part of life.

About 23 million people lived in the country. Most still worked on farms, but the United States was becoming a nation of industry. Many inventions, including the cotton gin, the telegraph, and the iron plow, made work and communication easier. Steamboats plied the rivers. Canals, roads, and nearly 9,000 miles (14,484 km) of railroad track crisscrossed the wilderness. New machinery made huge factories possible. Women no longer needed to weave their own fabrics. Instead, many went to work in the textile mills.

While some people grew rich running these businesses, workers earned very little. Other Americans also lived in the shadow of progress and prosperity. African Americans still labored on Southern plantations, but slavery was the subject of much disagreement. As women demanded more rights, an American was the first woman in the world to earn a medical degree. And Native Americans lost their lives and lands as settlers pushed anxiously west.

Dolley Madison's grave at Montpelier

presence, and to lend to it those charms with which she adorned the circle of the highest, the wisest, and best, during the bright career of her illustrious husband. Wherever she appeared, everyone became conscious of the presence of the spirit of benignity and gentleness, united to all the attributes of feminine loveliness."

Because Washington considered Dolley Madison "one of its own," she was buried in the Congressional Cemetery. Years later, however, Dolley's family moved her body next to James Madison in the family burial ground at Montpelier.

Within three years of Dolley's death, her house had been sold and its contents auctioned off. Payne had died of typhoid fever—alone in a Washington hotel. And Anna Payne Causten, who married a few months after Dolley's death, had died less than a year after Payne Todd. Although most physical aspects of Dolley Madison's life had disappeared by 1852, the memories and spirit of her contributions to her country remained alive. Like other great patriots of her day, Dolley Madison nurtured a lifetime relationship with the public and altered her nation's history in a positive way.

In 1962, on what would have been Dolley Madison's 194th birthday, collectors assembled memorabilia from Dolley Madison's life and presented the collection to the Greensboro Historical Museum in Greensboro, North Carolina. Today, the Dolley Madison Collection remains on exhibit as a permanent memorial to her.

☆ ☆ ☆ ☆ ☆ ☆ ☆ ☆ ☆ ☆ ☆ ☆ ☆ ☆

Dolley Payne Todd Madison
Timeline

1751	★	James Madison is born
1752	★	Liberty Bell is cast
1768	★	Dolley Payne is born on May 20
1770	★	Payne family buys Scotchtown estate in Virginia
1774	★	First Continental Congress meets in Philadelphia
1775	★	First shots of the Revolutionary War are fired at Lexington and Concord in Massachusetts
		Second Continental Congress meets in Philadelphia
1776	★	Declaration of Independence is signed
1777	★	Congress authorizes the Stars and Stripes as the American flag
1780	★	Pennsylvania abolishes slavery
1781	★	Articles of Confederation are ratified as a framework for governing the United States
		British surrender at Yorktown
1783	★	Dolley Payne's family moves to Philadelphia
		Treaty of Paris ends the Revolutionary War and Great Britain recognizes the independence of the United States
1787	★	Constitutional Convention is held in Philadelphia
1788	★	Constitution is ratified by a majority of states
		New York City becomes the nation's capital
1789	★	George Washington is inaugurated president
1790	★	First U.S. census determines the country's population to be 3,929,625
		Dolley Payne marries John Todd
		Philadelphia becomes the nation's capital

1791	★	Bill of Rights is ratified
1792	★	Dolley Payne Todd's son, John Payne Todd, is born
		Construction begins on the President's House
		George Washington is reelected president
1793	★	Dolley Payne Todd's son, William Temple, is born
		John Todd and William Temple Todd die
1794	★	Dolley Payne Todd marries James Madison
1796	★	John Adams is elected president
1799	★	George Washington dies
1800	★	U.S. population is 5,308,483
		The government moves to Washington, D.C.
		Thomas Jefferson is elected president
1801	★	Dolley Madison begins serving as President Jefferson's official hostess
1803	★	United States purchases Louisiana Territory from France
1804	★	Lewis and Clark expedition begins
		Thomas Jefferson is reelected president
1807	★	British navy impresses American seamen
		African slave trade is prohibited
1808	★	James Madison is elected president
1810	★	U.S. population is 7,239,881
1811	★	James Madison restricts trade with Great Britain
1812	★	United States declares war on Great Britain
		James Madison is reelected president
1813	★	U.S. Navy defeats the British on Lake Erie
1814	★	Dolley Madison saves valuable documents at the President's House before the British invade and burn Washington, D.C.
		Francis Scott Key writes "The Star-Spangled Banner"
		Treaty of Ghent officially ends the War of 1812

1815	★	Andrew Jackson wins the Battle of New Orleans after the war had officially ended
1816	★	James Monroe is elected president
1817	★	The Madisons retire to Montpelier
1818	★	United States and Britain agree on a permanent border between the United States and part of Canada at the 49th parallel
1819	★	United States buys Florida from Spain
1820	★	U.S. population is 9,638,453 James Monroe is reelected president
1821	★	First Americans settle in Mexican-controlled territory of Texas
1823	★	Monroe Doctrine proclaims the Americas off-limits to European powers
1824	★	John Quincy Adams becomes president after a disputed election

1825	★	Erie Canal opens, connecting New York City to cities on the Great Lakes
1826	★	John Adams and Thomas Jefferson die on July 4
1828	★	Andrew Jackson is elected president Noah Webster's *The American Dictionary of the English Language* is published
1829	★	*Encyclopedia Americana*, the first U.S. encyclopedia is published Englishman James Smithson leaves money to found the Smithsonian Institution in Washington, D.C.

1830	★	U.S. population is 12,866,020
1831	★	James Monroe dies
1832	★	Andrew Jackson is reelected president
1833	★	Oberlin College becomes the first to admit women
1835	★	Samuel Morse builds the first telegraph
1836	★	James Madison dies Martin Van Buren is elected president

1837	★	Economic depression spreads throughout the United States
		Dolley Madison moves back to Washington, D.C.
1840	★	U.S. population is 17,069,453
		William Henry Harrison is elected president
1841	★	William Henry Harrison dies a month after taking office
		John Tyler becomes president
1844	★	James Polk is elected president
1845	★	Andrew Jackson dies
1846	★	United States declares war on Mexico
		United States annexes New Mexico from Mexico
		John Deere constructs a steel plow
		Oregon Territory is divided between the United States and Britain at the 49th parallel
1847	★	U.S. Army captures Mexico City
		Smithsonian Institution is formally dedicated
1848	★	Treaty of Guadalupe Hidalgo ends the Mexican War and gives most of the present-day Southwest to the United States
		First U.S. women's rights meeting is held in Seneca Falls, New York
		Gold is discovered in California
		First medical school for women is opened in Boston, Massachusetts
		Zachary Taylor is elected president
		John Quincy Adams dies
1849	★	Thousands of people take part in the California gold rush
		Elizabeth Blackwell becomes the first woman in the world to receive a medical degree
		James Polk dies
		Dolley Payne Todd Madison dies on July 12

Fast Facts About
Dolley Payne Todd Madison

Born: May 20, 1768, in Guilford, North Carolina

Died: July 12, 1849

First Burial Site: Congressional Cemetery

Permanent Burial Site: Montpelier

Parents: John Payne and Mary Coles Payne

Education: Quaker schools

First Marriage: To John Payne on January 7, 1790, until his death in 1793

Second Marriage: To James Madison on September 15, 1794, until his death in 1836

Children: John Payne Todd and William Temple Todd

Places She Lived: Bird Creek, Scotchtown, and Coles Hill plantations in Virginia (1770–1783); Philadelphia (1783–1797); Montpelier (1797–1801, 1817–1837); Washington, D.C. (1801–1817, 1837–1849)

Major Achievements:

⋆ Set the standard for fashion and entertaining in Philadelphia and Washington, D.C.

⋆ Served as official hostess at the President's House for President Thomas Jefferson and became the first person to serve ice cream there

⋆ Set the standard for future First Ladies while First Lady for her husband President James Madison by decorating the President's House and holding conversation-filled dinner parties

⋆ Oversaw the wedding of her sister Lucy Payne Washington to U.S. Supreme Court Associate Justice Thomas Todd (March 29, 1812), the first wedding held in the President's House

⋆ Saved the Gilbert Stuart portrait of George Washington and important documents before the British burned the President's House during the War of 1812

⋆ Helped her husband prepare his presidential papers and sold them to Congress after his death

Fast Facts About
James Madison's Presidency

Terms of Office: Elected in 1808 and reelected in 1812; served as the fourth president of the United States from 1809 to 1817

Vice Presidents: George Clinton (1809–1812) and Elbridge Gerry (1813–1814); both men died in office and new vice presidents were not appointed

Major Policy Decisions and Legislation:
* Issued a proclamation in 1809 that reopened trade with Great Britain and later that year issued another proclamation once again stopping trade with Great Britain
* Signed a law in 1810 that banned British and French warships from U.S. waters
* Sent a war message to Congress in 1812 with reasons for declaring war on Britain and received support from Congress, which led to the War of 1812
* Recommended a federal network of roads and canals to Congress in his 1815 State of the Union Address
* Suggested that Congress consider a national bank in his 1816 State of the Union Address

Major Events:
* Joseph Story and Gabriel Duval are appointed as associate justices on the U.S. Supreme Court in 1811
* Louisiana is admitted as the eighteenth state on April 30, 1812
* War of 1812 is fought between the United States and Great Britain from July 1812 to January 1815
* Treaty of Ghent is signed December 14, 1814, ending the War of 1812
* Americans win the Battle of New Orleans on January 8, 1815, after the War of 1812 had officially ended
* Indiana is admitted as the nineteenth state on December 11, 1816

Where to Visit

Greensboro Historical Museum, the Dolley Madison Collection
20 Summit Avenue
Greensboro, North Carolina 27405

Montpelier (Madison's Home)
Montpelier Station, Virginia 22957

Greensboro Public Library
201 North Green Street
Greensboro, North Carolina 27401
(910) 373-2471

James Madison Museum
129 Caroline Street
Orange, Virginia 22960
(540) 672-1776

The White House
1600 Pennsylvania Avenue
Washington, D.C. 20500

Independence National Historical Park and Independence Hall
Chestnut Street between 5th and 6th Streets
Philadelphia, Pennsylvania

Library of Congress
Cutts Collection and Collection of Mrs. J. Madison Cutts III
Capitol Hill, 1st and Independence, SE
Washington, D.C. 20540

Jackson Library
College Avenue
The University of North Carolina at Greensboro
Greensboro, North Carolina 27412-5201
(910) 334-5880

Online Sites of Interest

The White House

http://www.whitehouse.gov/WH/Welcome.html

Information about the current president and vice president; White House history and tours; biographies of past presidents and their families (including biographies of James Madison and Dolley Payne Todd Madison); a virtual White House library; current events, and much more

The White House for Kids

http://www.whitehouse.gov/WH/kids/html/kidshome.html

Socks the cat is your guide to this site, which includes information about White House kids, past and present; famous "First Pets," past and present; historic moments of the presidency; several issues of a newsletter called "Inside the White House," and more

James Madison Museum

http://www.gemlink.com/~jmmuseum/

Visit this museum in Orange, Virginia, which features one of the nation's most outstanding collections of James and Dolley Madison memorabilia. The Madison exhibits include James Madison's favorite chair and many personal items that belonged to James and Dolley. Also on exhibit are furniture, antique farm tools, and Orange County memorabilia—including a 1931 fire truck. The museum's gift shop includes books about James Madison, writings by Madison, books about the Constitution, and Virginia Travel guides. Includes links to other Virginia sites and a link to the papers of James Madison

Virginia Online!

http://www.virginia.com

Sign the guestbook, visit local websites, check the weather forecast; dozens of links to a wide variety of Virginia sites, including a music site that features Virginia music, interviews with musicians, and a concert calendar

The Virginia Online History Project

http://www.inmind.com/people/shammer/history.htm

This site documents Virginia's rich history; includes many community histories, places and events, people; special collections and archives. Links to many sites.

Gateway Virginia

http://www.gateway-va.com/

Links to dozens of Virginia tourism, history, and current event sites.

For Further Reading

Brill, Marlene Targ. *Building the Capitol City*. Cornerstones of Freedom series. Danbury, CT: Children's Press, 1996.

Carter, Alden R. *The War of 1812: The Second Fight for Independence*. New York: Franklin Watts, 1992.

Clinton, Susan. *James Madison: Fourth President of the United States*. Encyclopedia of Presidents series. Chicago: Childrens Press, 1986.

Fradin, Dennis Brindell. *Virginia*. From Sea to Shining Sea series. Chicago: Childrens Press, 1992.

Davidson, Mary Richmond. *Dolley Madison*. Famous First Ladies series. New York: Chelsea Juniors, 1992.

Hargrove, Jim. *Thomas Jefferson: Third President of the United States*. Encyclopedia of Presidents series. Chicago: Childrens Press, 1986

Kent, Deborah. *The White House*. Cornerstones of Freedom series. Chicago: Children's Press, 1994.

Quackenbush, Robert. *James Madison and Dolley Madison and Their Times*. New York: Pippin Press, 1992.

Quiri, Patricia Ryon. *Dolley Madison*. New York: Franklin Watts, 1993.

Waters, Kate. *The Story of the White House*. New York: Scholastic, 1991.

Index

Page numbers in **boldface type** indicate illustrations

popularity of, 24, 26, 38, 63, 65, 79, 89

portraits of, **44, 47, 64, 78, 83**

as president, 57, 61, 65, 66

retirement to Montpelier, 51, **52,** 79, 81, 83, **81**

as secretary of state, 52

during War of 1812, 66, 68, 71, 73

Madison, Nellie (mother-in-law), 51

Madison papers, 81, 82, 83, 85

Monroe, James, 49, 75, 79, **80,** 81

inauguration of, 79

as secretary of state, 80

as secretary of war, 80

Montpelier, 44, 47, 51, **52,** 79, **81,** 90–91, **91**

burial of Madisons at, **84, 94,** 95,

sale of, 91

Mother Amy, 14, 19, 21

death of, 37

Mount Vernon, 34, 45

N

Native Americans, 65, 72

New Orleans, Battle of, 76, **76,** 85

New York City, 33, 35

Northwest Territory, 65

O

Octagon, 74, **74,** 75, **77**

"Oh, Susanna," 93

Old State House Bell, 29, **29.** *See also* Liberty Bell

Oregon Trail, The, 93

P

Paris, Treaty of (1783), 18

Payne, Anna (niece). *See*

Causten, Anna Payne (niece)

Payne, Anna (sister), 15, **20,** 21, 51, 53, 55

Payne, Dolley. *See* Madison, Dolley Payne Todd

Payne, Isaac (brother), 15, 21, 51

Payne, John (brother), 15, 21, 38

Payne, John (father), 13–14

bankruptcy of, 31

death of, 37, 39

as Quaker minister, 13–14

as small business owner, 21

Payne, Lucy (sister), 15, 37, 38, 66

Payne, Mary (sister), 15, 38, 51, 55

Payne, Mary Coles (mother), 13–14

death of, 55

decision to take in boarders, 31, **31**

move to Harewood estate, 38

nursing of Dolley by, 38

Payne, Philadelphia (sister), 28

Payne, Walter (brother), 14, 28

Payne, William Temple (brother), 14, 38, 51

Payne family

life in Virginia, 13–14, 17,19

move to Philadelphia, 19, 21, 26

opposition to slavery, 17, 19

in Revolutionary War, 17

Penn, William, 15

Pennsylvania, 15, 21–22

Philadelphia, *See also* Colonial America
19, 21–24, 29,

as capital, 22, **27,** 29, 35, **35**

colonial life in, 16, 21–24, **22,** 35–37, **36**

Constitutional Convention in, 42, 43, 82

institutions in, 22, **22**

library in, 22, **28**

population in, 22

Quaker meetings in 15, **15, 30**

return of Congress to, 33, 35

yellow fever outbreak in, 37, **37, 38**

Pine Street Meeting House, 26, 31, 33, **34**

monthly meeting in, 26

plantation system, 19

Plymouth Rock, 19

political parties, 42, 44, 50, 52, 85

Potomac River, 75

President's House, 53, 54, 57, **58, 75,** 87, 89. *See also* White House

after fire of 1814, 75, **75**

British attempt to destroy in War of 1812, **11,** 71, **71,** 73, **73**

East Room in, **70**

furnishing, 57, 58, **60**

official china of, **60**

restoration of, 59, 73, 74, 75, 76

social life at, 61, **61**

State Dining Room in, **59**

Q

Quakers, 13–14, **14**

beliefs of, 15–17, 19

clothing style of, **14,** 16, **18**

education for, 15, 24, **26**

meetinghouses for, **30,** 31 33, **34**

meetings of, 15, **15**

opposition to slavery, 14, 15, 17, 19
role of clerks in, 13–14
treatment of, nonbelivers, 37, 44, 49
wedding customs for, 37

R

Republican Party, 44, 50, 51
Revolutionary War, 16, 17, 22, 43, 80
causes of, 16
and Daughters of Liberty, 39
facts on, 18

S

Scotchtown, 14, **17**
Seneca Falls Conference, 39
slavery, 14, 16, 17, 19, 93
Quaker opposition to, 14, 15, 17, 19
Society of Friends. *See* Quakers
State House, 24, **27**, 42. *See also* Independence Hall
Stuart, Gilbert, 70
portrait of Washington by, 68, **70**
Sukey (maid), 68, 73

T

Tayloe House (Octagon), 74, **74**, 75
Taylor, Zachary, as president, 9
Todd, Dolley. *See* Madison, Dolley Payne Todd
Todd John, Jr. (first husband), 26, 33, 35, 38, 49
courtship of Dolley, 26
death of, from yellow fever, 38, 44

law practice of, 35
marriage of, to Dolley, 31
Todd, John Payne (son), 38, 44, 46, 53, **55**, 66, 68, 77
birth of, 36–37
death of, 95
education of, 55
financial problems of, 83, 92
life at Montpelier, 79, 83, 85, 90
return from Europe, 77
social life of, 83
Todd, William Temple (son), 38
typhoid fever, 95

U

U.S. Constitution, 35, 42, 43, 81
U.S. Navy, 66
U.S. Peace Commission, 77

V

Van Buren, Martin, 84, 87

W

War of 1812, 66–69, **70**, 71–77
Battle of Lake Champlain in, 66, **67**
Battle of Lake Erie in, 66, **72**
Battle of New Orleans in, 75, 76, **76**, 85
causes of, 65, 72
destruction of Washington, D.C., **10**, 11, **11**, 68, 71, **71**, 73, **73**
facts on, 72
Washington, D.C., 35, 53, **54**, 75
construction of, 53, 75

destruction of, in War of 1812, **10**, 11, 68, 71, **71**, 73, **73**
rebuilding of Capitol in, after War of 1812, 59, 75, 76
social life in, 53, 55
Washington, George, 23, 34, 37, **43**, 44, 45, 50, 62
as commander of Continental army, 34, 45
at Constitutional Convention, **43**
as Federalist, 50
as first president, 9, 34, 35, 62
as member of Continental Congress, 23
at Mount Vernon, 34, 45
saving of Stuart portrait of, by Dolley, **10**, 11, 68, 70, **70**
Washington, George Steptoe (brother-in-law), 37, 38, 46
Washington, Martha Dandridge Curtis, 44, 45, **45**, 50, 55
White House, **70**, **90**. *See also* President's House
Winder, William Henry, 66
Windsor chair, 36, **36**
women, in American Revolution, 39
women's movement, 39, 93

Y

"Yankee Doodle," 14
yellow fever epidemic, 37, **37**, 38
Yorktown, battle of, 18

Photo Credits©

About the Author

Alice Flanagan lives in Chicago, Illinois, and writes books for children for a variety of publishers. She credits her interest in history and her love of reading to her parents, who are avid readers and history buffs. Once a teacher, Ms. Flanagan knows the importance of having good books to stimulate reading and learning. Through her writing, she tries to provide those books and encourage an enthusiastic curiosity about life.

Ms. Flanagan has written many books for Children's Press. *Dolley Payne Todd Madison* is her first title in the Encyclopedia of First Ladies series. Other titles include *Rachel Donelson Jackson*, *Ellen Louise Axson Wilson*, and *Edith Bolling Galt Wilson*. Ms. Flanagan has written three titles in the Encyclopedia of Presidents series: *Andrew Jackson*, *Woodrow Wilson*, and *Franklin D. Roosevelt*. She has written numerous titles in the popular True Book series. Among her more recent titles is a five-book set on Native Americans: *The Pueblo*, *The Zuni*, *The Ute*, *The Shawnee*, and *The Wampanoag*.

Ms. Flanagan is also author of more than fifteen titles in the *Our Neighborhood* series for the primary grades. She likes this series because she had the opportunity to interview the people she wrote about. Also, she enjoyed working with her sister and her husband, who provided the photographs for this photojournalistic approach to career biographies.

Ms. Flanagan hopes young readers will like her book on Dolley Payne Todd Madison and be encouraged to find out more about Dolley Madison and the women who influenced history.